Planning for Learning through Pirates

by Marianne Sargent. Illustrated by Cathy Hughes

Contents

Published by Practical Pre-School Books, A Division of MA Education Ltd,
St Jude's Church, Dulwich Road, Herne Hill, London, SE24 0PB Tel: 020 7738 5454

www.practicalpreschoolbooks.com

© MA Education Ltd 2014

Front cover image © Lesya_boyko/Shutterstock.com
Back cover images (left-right) © Mariia Mykhaliuk/Shutterstock.com, Lucie Carlier © MA Education Ltd.

Planning for Learning through Pirates: ISBN: 978-1-909280-75-5

Making plans

Child-friendly planning

The purpose of planning is to make sure that all children enjoy a broad and balanced experience of learning. Planning should be flexible, useful and child-friendly. It should reflect opportunities available both indoors and outside. Plans form part of a planning cycle in which practitioners make observations, assess and plan.

Children benefit from reflective planning that takes into account the children's current interests and abilities and also allows them to take the next steps in their learning. Plans should make provision for activity that promotes learning and a desire to imagine, observe, communicate, experiment, investigate and create.

Plans should include a variety of types of activity. Some will be adult-initiated or adult-led that focus on key skills or concepts. These should be balanced with opportunities for child-initiated activity where the children take a key role in the planning. In addition, there is a need to plan for the on-going continuous provision areas such as construction, sand and water, malleable materials, small world, listening area, book area, role play and mark-making. Thought also needs to be given to the enhanced provision whereby an extra resource or change may enable further exploration, development and learning.

Furthermore, the outdoor environment provides valuable opportunities for children's learning. It is vital that plans value the use of outdoor space.

The UK Frameworks

Within the UK a number of frameworks exist to outline the provision that children should be entitled to receive. Whilst a variety of terms and labels are used to describe the Areas of Learning, there are key principles which are common to each document. For example, they advocate that practitioners' planning should be personal, based on observations and knowledge of the specific children within a setting. They acknowledge that young children learn best when there is scope for child-initiated activity. In addition, it is accepted that young children's learning is holistic and although Areas of Learning are presented separately withing each framework, in reality children's activities and explorations cross over and combine with different subject areas. Thus the Areas of

Learning are perhaps of most use for planning, assessment and recording to ensure that key areas are not overlooked.

Focused area plans

The plans you make for each day will outline areas of continuous provision and focused, adult-led activities. Plans for focused-area activities need to include aspects such as:

- Resources needed
- The way in which you might introduce activities
- Individual needs
- The organisation of adult help
- Size of the group
- Timing
- Safety
- Key vocabulary
- Key questions.

Identify the learning and the Early Learning Goals that each activity is intended to promote. Make a note of any assessments or observations that you are likely to carry out. After carrying out the activities, make notes on your plans to say what was particularly successful, or any changes you would make next time.

A final note

Planning should be seen as flexible. Not all groups meet every day, and not all children attend every day. Any part of the plan can be used independently, stretched over a longer period or condensed to meet the needs of any group. You will almost certainly adapt the activities as children respond to them in different ways and bring their own ideas, interests and enthusiasms. The important thing is to ensure that the children are provided with a varied and enjoyable curriculum that meets their individual developing needs.

Making plans

Using the book

Read the section which outlines links to the Early Learning Goals (pages 4-6) and explains the rationale for focusing on 'Pirates'.

The chart on page 7 gives an example format for weekly planning. It provides opportunity to plan for the on-going continuous provision, as well as more focused activities.

Use pages 8 to 19 to select from a wide range of themed, focused activities that recognise the importance of involving children in practical activities and giving them opportunities to follow their own interests.

For each 'Pirates' theme, two activities are described in detail as examples to help you in your planning and preparation. Key vocabulary, questions and learning opportunities are identified.

Use the activities as a basis to:

- Extend current and emerging interests and capabilities
- Engage in sustained conversations
- Stimulate new interests and skills.

Find out on page 20 how the 'Pirates' activities can be brought together with the 'Shipwrecked!' role play.

Use page 21 for ideas of resources to collect or prepare. Remember that the books listed are only suggestions. It is likely that you will already have within your setting a variety of other books that will be equally useful.

The activity overview chart on page 23 can be used either at the planning stage or after each theme has been completed. It will help you to see at a glance which aspects of children's development are being addressed and alert you to the areas which may need greater input in the future.

As children take part in the activities, their learning will progress. 'Collecting evidence' on page 22 explains how you might monitor each child's achievements.

There is additional material to support the working partnership of families and children in the form of a reproducible 'Family page' found inside the back cover.

It is important to appreciate that the ideas presented in this book will only be a part of your planning. Many activities that will be taking place as routine in your group may not be mentioned. For example, it is assumed that sand, dough, water, puzzles, role play, floor toys, technology and large scale apparatus are part of the ongoing early years experience. Role-play areas, stories, rhymes, singing, and group discussion times are similarly assumed to be happening in each week although they may not be a focus for described activities.

Using the 'Early Learning Goals'

The principles that are common to each of the United Kingdom curriculum frameworks for the early years are described on page 2. It is vital that, when planning for children within a setting, practitioners are familiar with the relevant framework's content and organisation for areas of learning. Regardless however, of whether a child attends a setting in England, Northern Ireland, Scotland or Wales they have a right to provision for all areas of learning. The children should experience activities which encourage them to develop their communication and language; personal, social, emotional, physical, mathematical and creative skills. They should have opportunities within literacy and be encouraged to understand and explore their world.

Within the Statutory Framework for the Early Years Foundation Stage (2014), Communication and Language; Physical Development and Personal, Social and Emotional Development are described as Prime Areas of Learning that are 'particularly crucial for igniting children's curiosity and enthusiasm for learning, and for building their capacity to learn, form relationships and thrive' (page 7, DfE 2014). The Specific Areas of Learning are Literacy, Mathematics, Understanding the World and Expressive Arts and Design.

For each area of learning, the Early Learning Goals (ELGs) describe what children are expected to be able to do by the time they enter Year 1. These goals, detailed on pages 4 to 6, have been used throughout this book to show how the activities relating to 'Pirates' aim to help children meet these expectations. For example, for Personal, Social and Emotional Development, one aspect relates to the development of children's 'self-confidence and self-awareness'. Activities aimed at helping children develop in this area have the reference PSE1. This will enable you to see which of the Early Learning Goals are covered for a given theme and to plan for areas to be revisited and developed.

In addition, an activity may be carried out to develop a range of areas of learning. For example, when the children build a role-play pirate ship they will use gross motor skills when moving and placing equipment, they will develop personal, social and emotional skills while working together, and they will develop their knowledge of expressive arts and design, during the build and later when using it during their play. Thus, whilst focused adult-led activities may have clearly defined goals at the planning stage, it must be remembered that as children take on ideas and initiate their own learning and activities, goals may change.

The Prime Areas of Learning

Communication and Language

Listening and attention: children listen attentively in a range of situations. They listen to stories, accurately anticipating key events and respond to what they hear with relevant comments, questions or actions. They give their attention to what others say and respond appropriately, while engaged in another activity. (CL1)

Understanding: children follow instructions involving several ideas or actions. They answer 'how' and 'why' questions about their experiences and in response to stories or events. (CL2)

Speaking: children express themselves effectively, showing awareness of listeners' needs. They use past, present and future forms accurately when talking about events that have happened or are to happen in the future. They develop their own narratives and explanations by connecting ideas or events. (CL3)

'Pirates' activities provide many opportunities for children to practice listening, understanding and speaking. By learning pirate language and sayings, children are extending their vocabulary, opening up more opportunities to use language when imagining and re-creating roles and experiences in their play. When playing the treasure hunt game in Theme 4 and flag action game in Theme 2, the children are required to listen to, understand and respond to instructions. They are also encouraged to use descriptive language during a treasure feely-bag game in Theme 5 and while making flags out of different materials in Theme 2. Furthermore, in Theme 6 they meet a 'real' pirate and use their communication skills to try to help him/her find his/her treasure by asking questions and sharing ideas.

Physical Development

Moving and handling: children show good control and coordination in large and small movements. They move confidently in a range of ways, safely negotiating space. They handle equipment and tools effectively, including pencils for writing. (PD1)

Health and self-care: children know the importance for good health of physical exercise, and a healthy diet, and talk about ways to keep healthy and safe. They manage their own basic hygiene and personal needs successfully, including dressing and going to the toilet independently. (PD2)

'Pirates' offers many opportunities for children to enjoy movement activities and handle tools and equipment. Making salt dough sea monsters in Theme 3 and threading jewels in Theme 5 improves fine motor control. Also, when making a real, working flag pole in Theme 2, children practice safely handling tools and construction materials. They gain physical confidence by walking the plank and climbing the ship's rigging in Theme 1 and improve their coordination through playing battleships and 'Capture the flag'. Children also experiment with ways of moving when playing a 'Treasure Island' game in Theme 4. Furthermore, they learn about becoming ill with scurvy at sea and find out why it is so important to eat a healthy diet that is rich in vitamin C.

Personal, Social and Emotional Development

Self-confidence and self-awareness: children are confident to try new activities, and say why they like some activities more than others. They are confident to speak in a familiar group, will talk about their ideas, and will choose the resources they need for their chosen activities. They say when they do or don't need help. (PSE1)

Managing feelings and behaviour: children talk about how they and others show feelings, talk about their own and others' behaviour and its consequences, and know that some behaviour is unacceptable. They work as part of a group or class, and understand and follow the rules. They adjust their behaviour to different situations, and take changes of routine in their stride. (PSE2)

Making relationships: children play co-operatively, taking turns with others. They take account of one another's ideas about how to organise their activity. They show sensitivity to others' needs and feelings, and form positive relationships with adults and other children. (PSE3)

It is possible to use 'Pirates' as a gateway theme through which to explore personal, social and emotional issues. In Theme 2 children consider the nature of piracy and what it involves, opening up discussion about right and wrong. In Theme 5 they are asked to think about things they treasure in life and in Theme 2 they are encouraged to express their feelings using flags. Pirates are used as a springboard for discussion about being gentle in play and sharing with each other, as well as to express positive thoughts about friends and peers. Furthermore, the term 'peg leg' is explained in Theme 3 when the children are introduced to issues surrounding disability.

The Specific Areas of Learning

Literacy

Reading: children read and understand simple sentences. They use phonic knowledge to decode regular words and read them aloud accurately. They also read some common irregular words. They demonstrate understanding when talking with others about what they have read. (L1)

Writing: children use their phonic knowledge to write words in ways which match their spoken sounds. They also write some irregular common words. They write simple sentences which can be read by themselves and others. Some words are spelt correctly and others are phonetically plausible. (L2)

'Pirates' is an exciting theme, which helps practitioners to get children, and especially boys, excited about writing. Using classic story books, such as *We're Going on a Bear Hunt* by Michael Rosen and Helen Oxenbury in Theme 5, inspires children to make up their own stories and set up treasure hunts with written clues. In Theme 4 the children draw their own treasure maps, ascribing meaning to the marks they draw and write. They engage in shared writing in Theme 6 when they compose a sea shanty: an activity that builds their awareness of rhythm, rhyme and alliteration. In Theme 2 children draw on their knowledge of pirate behaviour and language to make up their own pirate mottos. All the time they are provided with purposeful reading and writing opportunities including building word banks, making and following maps, writing labels, drawing signs and naming ships. Finally, a geocaching activity in Theme 4 is used to inspire written communication as practitioners help children communicate with other early years settings via email.

Mathematics

Numbers: children count reliably with numbers from 1 to 20, place them in order and say which number is one more or one less than a given number. Using quantities and objects, they add and subtract two single-digit numbers and count on or back to find the answer. They solve problems, including doubling, halving and sharing. (M1)

Shape, space and measures: children use everyday language to talk about size, weight, capacity, position, distance, time and money to compare quantities and objects and to solve problems. They recognise, create and describe patterns. They explore characteristics of everyday objects and shapes and use mathematical language to describe them. (M2)

There are plenty of activities featuring 'Pirates' in this book that aim to help develop children's mathematical knowledge.

The activities in Theme 2 show how useful flags are for playing number, shape, size and colour games. In Theme 1, children count how many pirates it takes to sink a ship and in Theme 6 they practice counting with the use of die while playing a pirate version of snakes and ladders. Then, in Theme 3, they increase their understanding of number by firing cannon balls into numbered barrels and learn basic concepts underpinning addition and subtraction by ordering pirates to walk the plank. Children also take a closer look at real British coins in Theme 5 and become familiar with everyday language associated with monetary value. Furthermore, exploring pirate treasure is ideal for learning about colour, shape and pattern.

Understanding the World

People and communities: children talk about past and present events in their own lives and in the lives of family members. They know that other children don't always enjoy the same things, and are sensitive to this. They know about similarities and differences between themselves and others, and among families, communities and traditions. (UW1)

The world: children know about similarities and differences in relation to places, objects, materials and living things. They talk about the features of their own immediate environment and how environments might vary from one another. They make observations of animals and plants and explain why some things occur, and talk about changes. (UW2)

Technology: children recognise that a range of technology is used in places such as homes and schools. They select and use technology for particular purposes. (UW3)

The topic of 'Pirates' opens up opportunities for learning about a diverse range of subjects. For instance, in Theme 1 children find out about the parts of a ship, the roles of different crew members and the type of food pirates ate. This is further explored in Theme 4 when the children learn about the different animals that lived on pirate ships, including unusual pets as well as productive farm animals. They find out about the reason why seamen sang shanties and the types of instruments pirates were most likely to play. Pirate flags are used as tools for recording wind direction in relation to the points of a compass and treasure hunting provides opportunities for children to learn about maps. In Theme 4, children learn about technological equipment and its uses for mapping and navigation when they use a GPS device to go geocaching and find some real treasure. All the time the children are using factual books and the Internet to gather information and find out more.

Expressive Arts and Design

Exploring and using media and materials: children sing songs, make music and dance and experiment with ways of changing them. They safely use and explore a variety of materials, tools and techniques, experimenting with colour, design, texture, form and function. (EAD1)

Being imaginative: children use what they have learnt about media and materials in original ways, thinking about uses and purposes. They represent their own ideas, thoughts and feelings through design and technology, art, music, dance, role play and stories. (EAD2)

Children explore a wide variety of materials, tools and techniques as they draw and paint pictures of ships and sea monsters, as well as make treasure chests, flags, treasure maps, hats, telescopes and models of sea monsters.

They work on a large scale to create a role-play pirate ship in Theme 1, carefully choosing from a variety of resources and assessing them to see if they adequately serve particular purposes. In Theme 5 they create a sparkling treasure-inspired collage and in Theme 3 they make story boxes for small world pirate play.

Pirate sea shanties are used as inspiration for dance, music and movement in Theme 6 and the children are encouraged to use percussion instruments to emulate the sound of the sea.

Note

The Early Learning Goals raise awareness of key aspects within any child's development for each area of learning. It is important to remember that these goals are reached through a combination of adult and child-initiated activities within early years settings, as well as in the child's home. Thus, it is vital that goals are shared by practitioners and parents, and children are given every opportunity to develop throughout their Early Years Foundation Stage both in their setting and at home.

Example chart to aid planning in the EYFS

Week beginning:	Monday	Tuesday	Wednesday	Thursday	Friday
FOCUSED ACTIVITIES					
Focus Activity 1:					
Focus Activity 2:					
Stories and rhymes					
CONTINUOUS PROVISION (Indoor)					
Collage					
Construction (large)					
Construction (small)					
ICT					
Imaginative play					
Listening					
Malleable materials					
Mark making					
Painting					
Role play					
Sand (damp)					
Sand (dry)					
Water					
CONTINUOUS PROVISION (Outdoor)					
Construction					
Creative play					
Exploratory play					
Gross motor					
ENHANCED PROVISION (Indoor)					
ENHANCED PROVISION (Outdoor)					

Theme 1: Ship Ahoy!

Communication and Language
- Take the children to a large quiet space and ask them to lie on their backs with their eyes closed. Give them a sensory description to help them imagine what it is like to sail on a pirate ship. Describe: the wide expanse of dark blue rolling ocean and cloudless skies; the sounds of the lapping water, pirates singing and gulls crying; feeling the boat rocking; the salty smell of the sea and the musty stink of unwashed pirates; the taste of the sea spray. Change the scene and plunge the ship into a storm. Invite children to stand up and take over describing the scene. (CL1, 3)

Physical Development
- Put gym benches outside for the children to pretend to 'walk the plank'. Show them how to jump and land safely. (PD1, 2)
- Use the PE apparatus in the school hall or visit a playground to practice climbing up rope ladders just like the rigging on a pirate ship. (PD1)
- Play 'Battleships'. Set out two rows of gym mats, one each end of an open space. These represent the pirate ships. Line up a row of bowling pins across the front edge of each 'ship'. Divide the children in to two teams and give them some large balls. These represent cannon balls. The aim of the game is to roll and throw the balls to knock down the opposing team's pins. (PD1)

Personal, Social and Emotional Development
- Discuss the need to be gentle when playing pirates. Invite the children to suggest how they can play at being pirate 'baddies' without actually hurting each other. (PSE2)

Literacy
- List the parts of a pirate ship on pieces of card. Help the children to read out the labels then stick them on a large diagram of a ship. (L1)
- Find examples of pirate and ship names in story books and challenge the children to make up their own. (L1)

Mathematics
- Visit www.earlylearninghq.org.uk/pirate_game/Main.html to find an interactive pirate ship counting game. (M1)
- Float different sized boats in water and see how many toy pirates each can hold before it sinks. (M1, 2)

Understanding the World
- Read *Look Inside a Pirate Ship* by Minna Lacey. Identify the different parts of the ship. Find out how pirates lived and the roles of different crew members. Create a lift-the-flap pirate ship (see display, opposite). (UW1, 2)
- Find out what happens to food on a pirate ship (see activity below). (UW2)
- Challenge the children to make junk pirate ships that float. Talk about the different materials available and consider which are waterproof and more likely to float. Test the ships and ask the children to explain why they float or sink. (UW2)

Expressive Arts and Design
- Use large bricks or crates to build a role-play pirate ship outside (see activity opposite). (EAD1, 2)
- Draw and paint pirate ships. (EAD1)

Activity: Pirate grub

Learning opportunity: Develops an understanding of decay; talks about why things happen and how things work.

Early Learning Goal: Understanding the World. The world.

Resources: Tinned, jarred, dried, pickled and frozen foods;

fresh foods that can be preserved in this way; sterile jars; cooking pan; vinegar; tupperware; freezer.

Key vocabulary: Fresh, preserve, rot, decay, mould, store, tin, jar, preservative, freeze, cool, bacteria, seal, boil, dry, food poisoning, sickness, diarrhoea.

Organisation: Small groups.

What to do: Explain that pirates used to stay on their ships for weeks at a time. This meant storing food below deck for long periods. There was no way to keep the food fresh so it would go off very quickly and pirates often got ill with food poisoning.

Explain that all foods contain tiny organisms called bacteria. We cannot see these bacteria feeding off the food but we can see the food 'going off' or rotting. It is possible to stop or kill bacteria. This is called preserving the food. There are different methods of preservation.

Show the children some examples of preserved food and explain how each method works:

- Tinned and jarred: Food is boiled to kill all the bacteria then sealed inside a container while it is still boiling hot.
- Frozen: Food is frozen and the bacteria are frozen with it.
- Pickled: Some foods can be pickled in a liquid preservative such as vinegar that kills the bacteria.
- Dried: Some foods can be left to dry out. This also kills the bacteria or slows it to a stop. Dried meats are often coated in salt, which helps to draw the moisture out.

Prepare and taste the different types of preserved food. Talk about the texture and how it looks, tastes and smells.

Have a go at preserving some food to show the children what happens to it. For example, boil some pears and seal them in a jar. Leave them overnight to cool then open the jar and invite the children to try them. Compare them with fresh pears and note the difference in appearance, texture and taste. Have a go at freezing fruit, drying bananas and pickling beetroot.

Carry out some experiments to find out what happens to food when it is stored without being preserved. Leave some fruit in a bowl and observe it as it goes mouldy and rots. Leave some milk out of the fridge for a couple of days and see what happens to it.

Explain that when we eat food that has gone off, our bodies usually try to get rid of it and we suffer with sickness and diarrhoea. That is why it is important to store food properly.

Activity: Building a role-play pirate ship

Learning opportunity: Constructs with a purpose in mind, using a variety of resources; engages in imaginative role play.

Early Learning Goal: Expressive Arts and Design. Exploring and using media and materials. Being imaginative.

Resources: Large wooden blocks and planks; crates; cardboard boxes; brooms; benches; chairs; blankets; clothes airers; ropes; flags.

Key vocabulary: Build, construct, plan, shape, join, stern, bow, hull, mast, rigging, deck, plank, Ship Ahoy!, high seas, sailing, ocean, port, starboard, poop deck, quarterdeck.

Organisation: Small groups.

What to do: Challenge the children to build a role-play pirate ship using large construction materials and everyday objects. Encourage them to make their own suggestions about what they can use. Promote discussion about their different ideas as they work together to build their ship.

Once the ship is complete give the children time to play in it. Later, help them to evaluate their work by asking if there is anything they would like to change.

Display

Create a lift-the-flap pirate ship. Draw a large outline of a ship on thick card. Include a mast but not sails. Cut it out and use it as a stencil to draw another ship on white card. In pencil, divide the lower deck of the ship into parts, including a stowaway, sleeping area and galley. Invite children to draw pictures showing what is happening within each area inside the ship as well as on and around the mast.

Use the stencil to draw an identical outline of the ship on another piece of white card. Draw sails on this picture. This is going to be the outside of the ship and it will sit on top of the first piece of card. With a pencil, divide this picture into the same ship's areas as the first. Use this as a guide to mark out door flaps in black pen. Rub out the pencil marks then invite children to paint and draw details on the outside of the ship.

Use sharp scissors or a craft knife to cut open the flaps you marked out earlier. Cut around the sails to create more flaps that reveal the pirates on and around the mast underneath. Then, taking care not to put any glue on the flaps, stick the top card onto the bottom card. Finally, hang the picture on the wall at a height that will enable children to open and close the flaps independently.

Theme 2: Flying the Jolly Roger flag

Communication and Language
- Make a set of small pirate flags using different materials, for example corduroy, felt, sandpaper, corrugated card, tinfoil, silk and cellophane. Give the flags to the children to play with. Ask them to think about whether the materials work well for flags. Encourage them to describe the texture of each material and how it moves. (CL3)
- Use small hand-held pirate flags to play a listening game. Instruct the children to wave their flags up high, down low, to the right, to the left and behind their backs. Get them to swap flags with certain others, for example, boys, girls, children wearing red jumpers or children with black hair. (CL1, 2)

Physical Development
- Use small pirate flags to play physical games. For example; run around outside and wave the flags in the breeze; play Simon Says; or use red, orange and green flags as stop, walk and run signals. (PD1)
- Play a simple version of 'capture the flag'. Place a hula hoop at each end of an open space. Put five flags inside each hoop. Divide the children into two small teams. Explain that they must run to the other team's hoop, take one flag and race back to put it in their own hoop. The winning team is the one with the most flags in their hoop at the end. (PD1)
- Make a flag pole (see activity opposite). (PD1, 2)

Personal, Social and Emotional Development
- Use flags to communicate feelings during circle time or check-in at the beginning of the day. Use coloured flags to represent emotions, for example, red (angry), yellow (happy), blue (sad) and purple (tired). Otherwise use flags featuring smiley or sad skulls and crossbones. (PSE2)
- Use information books to find out about real pirates. Help the children to consider how pirates live and what they do (see activity opposite). (PSE2)

Literacy
- Give some examples of pirate mottos such as Black Bart's 'A merry life and a short one' or Jack Sparrow's 'Take what you can, give nothing back'. Talk about what they might mean. Another popular saying among pirates was 'No purchase, no pay', meaning if they did not plunder a ship they would not be paid.

Help the children make up their own pirate mottos to display with their flags (see display opposite). (L1, 2)

Mathematics
- Use flags to play number, colour and shape recognition games. For example, put different coloured flags in a large open space. When you call out a colour the children must run to the appropriate flag. Do the same with numbers and shapes. Invite the children to take turns at being the caller. (M1, 2)
- Make number flags featuring numerals and sets of pirate objects like skulls, ships, swords or parrots. Use these for number and counting activities. (M1)
- Make different sized flags for children to compare, measure and order. (M2)

Understanding the World
- Erect a pirate flag outside and use playground chalk to draw a compass showing North, South, East and West on the floor next to it. Take the children outside on breezy days to check the direction of the wind. (UW2)

Expressive Arts and Design

● Provide cheap white pillow cases and fabric pens for the children to design flags for the flag pole (see activity below). Punch holes into the top and bottom corners of each flag so that they can be attached to the pole and used in a role-play pirate ship. (EAD1)

Activity: What are pirates?

Learning opportunity: Talks about others' behaviour and its consequences.

Early Learning Goal: Personal, Social and Emotional Development. Managing feelings and behaviour.

Resources: Information books about pirates.

Key vocabulary: Pirate, piracy, theft, stealing, robbery, hijack, attack, ship, right, wrong, bounty, treasure, pistol, sword, hurt.

Organisation: Whole group.

What to do: Use information books to explain what pirates are and what they do. Begin by explaining that piracy is the practice of attacking and stealing from ships at sea:

Pirates are ocean robbers. The pirates we see in story books are based on what pirates used to look like three hundred years ago when they ruled the seas in huge galleons governed by a captain and quartermaster. They raided other ships armed with pistols and swords and stole any gold on board, as well as anything else that would be of use. This 'treasure' included food, drinking water, clothing, soap, alcohol (grog), rope, anchors and weapons. They often hijacked the whole ship, sent it away to be sold and made the crew join them to work on the pirate ship.

Ask the children to consider how they feel about piracy. What do they think about stealing? Do they think it is right or wrong? Can they explain why?

Activity: Making a flag pole

Learning opportunity: Handles tools, objects, construction and malleable materials safely and with increasing control.

Early Learning Goal: Physical Development. Moving and handling.

Resources: Old broom handle or thick wooden doweling; cellophane; tape; petroleum jelly; sand; trowel; cement; bucket; simple small pulley; thick string; cleat; child-sized manual hand drill; vice; screws; child-sized screwdriver; Jolly Roger flag with grommets (holes to tie the rope to).

Key vocabulary: Jolly Roger, flag, pole, raise, pulley, rope, drill, screw, screwdriver, vice, raise, lower, hoist.

Organisation: Small groups, choosing individual children to help with different parts of the process.

What to do: Invite a couple of children to help wrap cellophane around the bottom of a broom handle or doweling rod and secure it with tape. Ask them to coat the cellophane in petroleum jelly. Show the group how to mix cement. Choose one child to hold the cellophane coated end of the pole upright in the centre of a bucket. Help the other children fill in around the pole with the cement. Leave it to set overnight.

Remove the pole and ask the children to peel off the cellophane. Secure the pole in a vice and use a manual hand drill and screws to fasten a simple pulley to the top of the pole. Then attach the cleat about half way down the pole.

All the time, talk to the children about the tools and how to handle them safely. Allow them to have a go at using the drill and screwdriver.

Stand the pole back in the bucket and ask a child to thread a thick piece of string through the pulley. Help some children tie one end of the string to the grommet at the top of the flag then attach the other end of the string to the bottom grommet.

Pull the string through the pulley so that the flag rises up the pole. Wrap the loose hanging string around the cleat to hold it in place. Place the flag pole in the role-play pirate ship so the children can hoist and lower it during their play.

Display

Explain that the Jolly Roger flag depicting the skull and crossed bones was only one design of flag. It is the most well known because it has been used in many films, stories and toys.

Pirates actually flew all kinds of flags designed to scare. Some even had different coloured flags that were intended to send messages to the crew on target ships. Visit http://prints.rmg.co.uk/art/501119/A-selection-of-18th-pirate-flags

Provide white A5 paper and fabric crayons for the children to design their own scary pirate flag. Use an iron to transfer their designs onto some white cotton fabric. Attach the fabric flags to small pieces of doweling. Mount the flags on a wall display accompanied by the children's own pirate mottos.

Theme 3: A pirate's life

Communication and Language

- Read *The Pirate Cruncher* by Jonny Duddle. Go back to the beginning and re-read the letter. Take a closer look at the old fiddler. Do the children notice anything strange about him? Go back through the book a second time and ask them if they can spot the sea monster in any of the pictures. Are any of the children able to explain what happens to the pirates in the story? (CL1, 2, 3)

Physical Development

- Make salt dough sea monsters. Bake them, paint them and varnish them for use in small world play. (PD1)
- Explain that pirates were unable to keep fresh fruit and vegetables on their ships because they would rot (see activity in Theme 1). This meant pirates were at risk of becoming sick with a deadly illness called scurvy, which is caused by not taking in enough vitamin C. Use information books to find out which vitamins are found in different foods and what they do to keep the body healthy. (PD2)

Personal, Social and Emotional Development

- Talk about the term 'peg leg'. Pirates were at risk of losing a leg in battle, in an accident or through illness. Most pirates could not afford an artificial leg at all and would simply use crutches. However, those who could afford it would have a wooden peg leg because lifelike artificial legs were too expensive. Explain there are many people nowadays who have artificial legs. Modern technology is so good that these legs make it possible for disabled people to continue to undertake everyday tasks. What's more, some even go on to participate in competitive sport at the highest level. Show some footage of Paralympic athletes in action. Point out that calling someone with an artificial leg a 'peg leg' is considered an insult. (PSE3)

Literacy

- Provide plastic bottles, paper and pens for the children to send messages in bottles. Encourage the children to introduce storylines that may prompt use of the bottles in role play. (L1, 2)
- Make a pirate alphabet lotto game. Make boards featuring pictures of pirate objects and corresponding initial sound cards featuring the letters of the alphabet. (L1)

Mathematics

- Provide pirate clothing templates cut from card and ask the children to add colourful patterns. (M2)
- Wrap corrugated card around some buckets and paint them to look like barrels. Paint a number on each

barrel and line them up outside. Provide a bucket of black balls and challenge the children to fire the correct number of cannon balls into each barrel. (M1)
- Play washing line number, colour and pattern games with pirate socks. (M1, 2)
- Play a pirate-themed subtraction and addition game (see activity opposite). (M1)

Understanding the World

- Find out about the animals that lived on board a pirate ship (see activity opposite). (UW1, 2)

Expressive Arts and Design

- Show the children some pictures of sea monsters in story books. Use these as inspiration for the children to draw and paint their own. (EAD1)
- Provide shoe boxes and craft materials for the children to make pirate-themed story boxes for small world play. (EAD1)
- Make pirate hats with black card and telescopes out of kitchen rolls. (EAD1)

Activity: 'Walk the plank, you scurvy sea dog!'

Learning opportunity: In practical activities and discussion, is beginning to use the vocabulary involved in adding and subtracting.

Early Learning Goal: Mathematics. Number.

Resources: Brown and white card; marker pens; scissors; laminator; dice; white stickers.

Key vocabulary: How many left? How many altogether? Take away, count.

Organisation: Small groups.

What to do: Draw a set of four pirate ships, each with a plank sticking out and a ladder hanging down the side. Draw a set of 10 pirates and photocopy them so that you have a set for each ship. Invite some children to colour them. Cut out the ships and pirates and laminate them. Use stickers to replace numbers four, five and six on a numbered die with one, two and three, so that each number is shown twice.

Bring four children together to play a subtraction game. Give each child a pirate ship and a crew of 10 pirates. Ask each child to take a turn to roll the dice and make the corresponding number of pirates walk the plank off the ship.

Talk through what is happening each time. For example: There are six pirates on your ship and you have to make two walk the plank. How many pirates have you got left?

Towards the end the children must roll the exact number before they can make their remaining pirates jump off the ship. The first child to have an empty ship is the winner.

Play the game again, but this time the aim is to add pirates to the ship by getting them to climb a ladder and get back on board.

Activity: Animals on board

Learning opportunity: Show interest in different occupations and ways of life; talks about why things happen and how things work.

Early Learning Goal: Understanding the World. People and communities. The world.

Resources: Books about farm produce; examples of dairy and meat products; information books about domestic animals and exotic pets; information books about exotic animals and endangered species.

Key vocabulary: Animal, food, produce, meat, bacon, ham, pork, beef, chicken, dairy, milk, cheese, butter, eggs, mice, pest, disease, pet, cat, hunt, predator, capture, parrot, monkey, exotic, expensive, valuable.

Organisation: Small groups.

What to do: Tell the children that pirates took animals with them on their voyages. Farm animals such as goats, chickens and pigs were a popular choice because they were a source of fresh food. Goats produce milk, chickens lay eggs and both of these animals, as well as pigs can be eaten.

Provide examples of produce from farm animals, such as bacon, ham, eggs, beef burgers, cheese and milk. Ask the children if they can tell you which animals these products come from.

There were a lot of mice on pirate ships. Ask the children if they have any ideas why. Explain that mice spread disease and ask if they know why pirates kept cats on board.

Pirates also kept exotic animals including parrots and monkeys. They would either steal these animals from other ships or capture them on tropical islands. They would then take them home, where they could sell them as pets for a lot of money.

Introduce the topic of keeping exotic pets for discussion. Does anyone have an exotic pet at home? Do they have to do anything special to keep it happy, healthy and safe? Encourage the children to think about the needs of different animals. For example, a parrot needs plenty of room to fly and monkeys are very sociable and need space to climb.

Help the children to consider why some animals are happy to live with people as pets and some are not. Ask them if they can explain why capturing a wild animal and keeping it as a pet might not be a good idea.

Display

Use the children's drawings of sea monsters (see EAD) as inspiration and draw an outline of a sea monster on a large piece of medium-density fibreboard (MDF).

If possible, take the children to the seaside to collect natural collaging materials, including sand, small pebbles, shells, feathers, dried seaweed and smoothed glass. Help the children stick these found objects onto the MDF outline using PVA glue. Encourage them to think about the effects they are trying to create. Look at the colours of the objects and consider how sticking things on in particular ways can create form, shape and pattern. Look at individual objects and consider whether they can be used to represent specific features. For example, are there any objects that can be used to create scales, tentacles, suckers, teeth or eyes?

Display the collage on the wall as a permanent artwork.

Theme 4: 'X marks the spot'

Communication and Language

- Play a treasure hunt speaking and listening game with the children in pairs. Give one child a small treasure chest to hide. That child must then give their partner verbal instructions to find it. Encourage the children to use positional language and plenty of description. (CL1, 2, 3)
- Ask the children to describe their journey to the setting. Do they travel by foot or vehicle? What do they pass on the way? Which side of the road do they see these things? Draw a visual map of their journey. (CL3)

Physical Development

- Play 'Treasure Island'. Set this game up in a large open indoor space. Create a rugged landscape. For example: Lay a blue sheet across the middle of the floor to represent a lake with a gym bench across the middle to represent a bridge; set out cones to represent trees; use gym mats to represent a muddy bog. Place a tub of beanbags at the far side of the room. Talk through and explain the landscape to the children. Send them one at a time to collect a piece of treasure (beanbag) from the tub. Encourage them to weave in and out of the cones, walk across the bench, slither on their fronts across the blue sheet and crawl across the mats. (PD1)

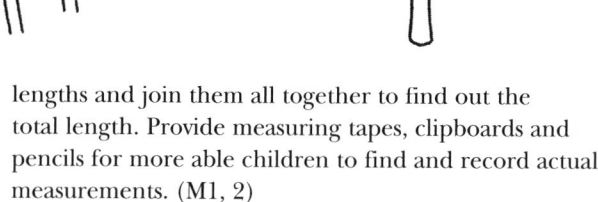

Personal, Social and Emotional Development

- Give a group of children some gold chocolate coins and challenge them to divide them up so everyone has a fair share. (PSE3)

Literacy

- Make treasure maps (see activity opposite). (L1, 2)
- Provide playground chalks for the children to draw maps on the floor outside. (L2)
- Correspond with your geocaching partner setting via email (see UW). Help children send messages about where they went and what they did. Attach photographs of the expedition. **Note:** Ensure you know and trust the staff in your partner setting. Remember to get parents' written consent before emailing photographs of their children. (L2)

Mathematics

- Set out a selection of wooden planks of varying lengths. Challenge the children to arrange them in size order, join different planks together to make equivalent lengths and join them all together to find out the total length. Provide measuring tapes, clipboards and pencils for more able children to find and record actual measurements. (M1, 2)
- Set up a sorting activity. Provide small chests filled with treasures that can be sorted by shape, colour, size and material. (M2)

Understanding the World

- Go geocaching (see activity opposite). (UW2, 3)
- Visit www.earlylearninghq.org.uk/themes/pirates/ pirate-themed-programmable-robot-mat/ to find a pirate map for use with a programmable toy. (UW3)
- Look at maps. Find countries on a globe or world map. Look at a map of the UK and identify where England, Scotland, Wales and Northern Ireland are. Find where relatives and friends live or come from. Look at a satellite map of the local area and locate familiar buildings known to the children. (UW2)

Expressive Arts and Design

- Make treasure maps for the role-play area. These can feature whatever places the children choose; desert islands, forests or cities. Show the children how to age their maps by scrunching them up, tearing them around the edges and staining them with damp teabags. (EAD1, 2)

Activity: Making treasure maps

Learning opportunity: Knows information can be relayed in the form of print; begins to read words; gives meaning to marks as they draw and write; uses phonic knowledge to write words.

Early Learning Goal: Literacy. Reading. Writing.

Resources: Example treasure maps; paper; pens, pencils, pencil crayons, felt pens; rulers; chocolate gold coins for treasure.

Key vocabulary: Map, treasure, draw, label, mark, plot, x marks the spot, find, landmark, guide, search.

Organisation: Small groups.

What to do: Show the children some example treasure maps. Point out the landmarks and read out the labels. Look for the X that marks the spot where the treasure is hidden.

Provide paper and drawing equipment for the children to make their own treasure maps featuring the setting. Encourage them to look around for landmarks. Point out doors, windows, cupboards and pieces of furniture that should be shown on the map. Help them label their maps.

Send the children off to hide their treasure. Then help them locate the hiding places on their maps and mark where their treasure is hidden with an X. Get the children to swap their maps with each other and use them to seek out each other's treasure.

Help less able children: Draw a sketch of the setting and photocopy it. Hand these out for the children to use as a basis for their maps.

Activity: Go geocaching

Learning opportunity: Comments and asks questions about aspects of the natural world; recognises that a range of technology is used for particular purposes in a variety of settings.

Early Learning Goal: Understanding the World. The world. Technology.

Resources: Pictures of satellites; computer; smart phone with compass app or GPS device.

Key vocabulary: Geocaching, search, map, satellite.

Organisation: Small groups.

What to do: Geocaches are treasure boxes that are created and hidden all over the world by the general public. They are tracked down using GPS enabled devices such as smart phones.

Set up a free account on a geocaching website, such as www.geocaching.com, where you will find very helpful videos and tutorials about how geocaching works. It helps to have a geocaching app on your phone. These apps provide GPS maps with locations of nearby geocaches, detailed descriptions of their locations and hints about how to find them. There are also notes from other geocachers who have already found them, which is especially useful because you can check up on the condition of a geocache, as well as find out if it has gone missing.

When geocaching with young children it is a good idea to set up your own geocache or partner up with other early years settings and hide them for each other. That way you can ensure the geocache is situated in an accessible area and the contents are suitable for young children. Always send an adult ahead to check the geocache before you search for it to ensure that it is still in place and the contents are still intact.

Once you have hidden a geocache and uploaded the details to a geocaching website it will usually take a couple of days for it to be verified, so make sure you forward plan.

Show the children images of satellites in space. Explain satellites send signals down to our computers and mobile phones. Take the children outside, hold a smart phone in the air and explain satellites are sending signals to it right now. Switch on the compass app on the phone and show the children the latitude and longitude readings. Explain these numbers are called coordinates. The phone is working with the satellites to figure out exactly where you are standing on planet Earth. This is called the Global Positioning System (GPS). Demonstrate how GPS works by going geocaching and finding your hidden treasure!

> **Internet safety:** Geocaching should be a safe activity as long as you partner up with a trusted setting and check the geocaches beforehand. However, there are always risks involved in using the Internet. Find advice on Internet safety from the UK Safer Internet Centre: www.saferinternet.org.uk.

> The National Trust holds free geocaching events for people who feel less confident about using this technology. Go to www.nationaltrust.org.uk/visit/activities/geo-caching/ for more information.

Display

Create a wall display about your geocaching expedition. Print out a map of the search area and mark the spot where the geocache was found. Display photographs of the children searching with speech bubbles featuring their questions and comments. Keep track of your geocache on the website and print off and display any comments that other geocachers make when they find yours.

Theme 5: Buried treasure

Communication and Language
- Gather a selection of treasure pieces, for example a necklace, jewels, gold coins and silverware. Choose one object at a time and hide it in a feely bag. Invite the children to take turns at feeling and describing what is inside the bag, while the other children guess what it is. (CL1, 2)
- Explain the meanings behind pirate language associated with treasure. For example, pieces of eight were silver coins used across the Spanish Empire. One of these coins was worth eight reales in Spanish old money or £50 in today's money. Doubloons were gold coins worth 32 reales. Source some pictures of these coins on the Internet to show the children. Other words include: loot, riches, spoils, plunder and lucre. (CL3)

Physical Development
- Make jewellery by threading plastic gems onto string. (PD1)
- Set up a tricky treasure hunt (see activity opposite). (PD1)
- Bury treasure deep in a sand pit and provide spades for the children to dig for it. (PD1)

Personal, Social and Emotional Development
- Read *Treasure Ahoy! Pirates Can Share* by Tom Easton and Mike Gordon. Pause part way through and ask the children to consider what Sam should do with the treasure he finds. Encourage the children to give reasons for their ideas and opinions. At the end of the story help the children to reflect upon Sam's actions. Do they think he did the right thing in the end? Why/ why not? (PSE2, 3)
- Introduce the idea of sentimental value to the children. Ask them if they have anything at home that they might describe as 'personal treasures'. Do they own anything really special that means a lot to them? (See Home Links.) (PSE2)

Literacy
- Use Michael Rosen's *We're Going on a Bear Hunt* as inspiration for making up your own treasure hunt version of the story (see activity opposite). (L1)
- Read *The Treasure Hunt* by Nick Butterworth. Provide some gold coins for the children to set up treasure hunts for each other. Help them set out a trail of picture clues just like Percy does in the story. Encourage more able children to compose written clues. (L1, 2)

Mathematics
- Make repeating patterns with jewels. (M2)
- Examine some real coins. Look at the shapes, colours and pictures. Tell the children the value of each coin. Play with the coins: press them into play dough; do rubbings; arrange them in order of size; arrange them in order of value; match up a single coin with the equivalent in coins of lower value. (M1, 2)

Understanding the World
- Visit the CBeebies website (www.bbc.co.uk/cbeebies/ swashbuckle-online/games/swashbuckle-adventures/) to find some 'Swashbuckle Adventures' pirate games that aim to improve the children's concentration, timing and mouse control. (UW3)
- Bury metal pieces of treasure in the sand tray or pit. Provide metal detectors to help the children find them. (UW3)
- Melt some chocolate and use a coin mould to make some chocolate coins. Talk about the changes taking place as the chocolate melts over heat and solidifies when cooled. (UW2)

Expressive Arts and Design

● Provide shoe boxes for the children to make treasure chests and shiny craft materials to make treasure. Allow the children to use their chests in the role-play area. (EAD1, 2)
● Provide sparkly craft materials for the children to make treasure inspired collages. (EAD1)

Activity: Tricky treasure hunt

Learning opportunity: Travels with confidence and skill around, under, over and through balancing and climbing equipment.

Early Learning Goal: Physical Development. Moving and Handling.

Resources: Gym benches; tunnels; crash mats; tables; slides; climbing frame; treasure (gems or coins).

Key vocabulary: Hunt, search, treasure, climb, slide, through, under, on, up, down, over, around.

Organisation: Small groups.

What to do: Set out a range of obstacles and climbing equipment in a large space inside or outdoors. Make sure the equipment is placed close together so that the children can climb from one thing to another without touching the floor. Place crash mats around the equipment then hide pieces of treasure everywhere, ensuring it does not pose a trip hazard.

Challenge the children to find the treasure. Explain they must climb over the equipment to reach it. They must not put their feet on the floor or they risk being caught by a crocodile (you!).

Activity: 'We're going on a treasure hunt'

Learning opportunity: Begins to be aware of the way stories are structured; suggests how the story might end; describes settings, events and characters.

Early Learning Goal: Literacy. Reading.

Resources: *We're Going on a Bear Hunt* by Michael Rosen and Helen Oxenbury; whiteboard or flip chart and pen.

Key vocabulary: Story, beginning, middle, end, setting, where, what, how, weather, place, feel, sound, see, hear, travel, scary, exciting.

Organisation: Small groups.

What to do: Read *We're Going on a Bear Hunt* to the children and explain that you are going to make up your own version about a treasure hunt.

Ask the children how they would like the story to begin. Who are the treasure hunters going to be, pirates or someone else after a pirate's treasure perhaps? Are the treasure hunters on sea or land? Do they set off from a ship or building? Point out that *We're Going on a Bear Hunt* is set on a 'beautiful day' and ask what kind of weather the children would like for their story setting.

Move on to the middle of the story. Do the treasure hunters travel by boat, vehicle or on foot? What kind of obstacles do they come across, shark infested waters, rough seas, rolling sand dunes, creepy forests, stinking swamps or dark caves? How might the weather affect the landscape? Encourage the children to come up with their own suggestions.

What about the ending? Ask the children what the treasure hunters should find at the end. Should it be something exciting or scary?

As you compose the story together, write it down on a whiteboard or flip chart. Then read each group's story out to everyone at the end of the session.

Extend the activity by working with each group to create a slide show version of their story using presentation software. (For inspiration, see an example on the TES Connect website: www.tes.co.uk/teaching-resource/We-and-39-re-Going-on-A-Treasure-Hunt-Pirates-6322882/event/22/).

Display

Set up some balance scales on a table and provide a basket of treasure for the children to play around with and find out what weighs more/less or is heavier/lighter. Include treasures that are made from a variety of materials, for example plastic and metal coins or glass and plastic jewels.

Display some questions, for example: Which coins are heavier? Which is the lightest jewel? Which piece of jewellery weighs the most?

Theme 6: Sea shanties

Communication and Language

- Visit the British Council website (http://learnenglishkids.british council.org/en/songs/the-pirates-song) to find a song that introduces a wide range of vocabulary associated with pirates. Play this to the children and introduce them to more pirate sayings and vocabulary that they can use to enhance their role play (see activity opposite). (CL1, 2, 3)
- Invite an adult to visit the setting dressed as a pirate. Make up a story about lost treasure and instruct the visitor to relay it to the children. Gather the children together to hear the pirate's tale of woe. Invite them to ask questions and share any ideas they might have about how to find the treasure. (CL1, 2, 3)

Physical Development

- Read *Port Side Pirates* by Oscar Seaworthy and Debbi Harter. Take the children to an open space and dance and sing-a-long to the accompanying CD while doing the actions. (PD1)
- Play musical pirates. Dress up as pirates and dance to pirate music. Each time the music stops the children must freeze. Any children still moving are out and must shout, 'You filthy land lubbers' as they leave the game. (PD1)

Personal, Social and Emotional Development

- Practice turn taking by passing a microphone around while singing pirate songs. Explain that the children can only sing if they have the microphone in their hand. (PSE1, 2)
- Ask the children to think of positive things they can say about their friends (shipmates). For example, choose a child and ask the others to think of nice words to describe him/her, such as friendly, fun or kind. Recite the following and encourage the children to fill in the blanks: Pirate _____ is a part of this crew, s/he is always _____ and seaworthy too! (PSE1, 2, 3)

Literacy

- Compose a pirate sea shanty (see activity opposite). (L1, 2)

Mathematics

- Read *Ten Little Pirates* by Mike Brownlow and Simon Rickerty. Line up 10 toy pirates and take one away each time a pirate comes to a sticky end. (M1)

- Use playground chalks to draw a large-scale, pirate-themed snakes and ladders game on the floor outside. Draw rope ladders and planks in place of snakes. Explain the children should use a large die to move themselves around the board. (M1)

Understanding the World

- Explain sailors had to work hard to keep their ship seaworthy, climbing rigging, adjusting sails, scrubbing the decks and keeping everything ship-shape. Singing kept their spirits up and special songs called sea shanties had rhythms that helped everyone all work together. A shantyman would lead everyone in their singing. (UW1)
- Music was important on a pirate ship because it helped to keep everyone happy. Musicians were respected and treated well. Look at examples of instruments that would be played on board a ship like the accordion, fiddle, drums and tin whistle. If possible, have a go at playing some. (UW1, 2)

Expressive Arts and Design

- Listen to a child-friendly version of *Yo Ho Ho and a Bottle of Rum* on YouTube (www.youtube.com/watch?v=CVHjfQ0JsVQ).
- Use percussion instruments to emulate the sound of calm and stormy seas. (EAD2)
- Clap to the beat and play musical instruments in time to a sea shanty. (EAD2)

Activity: Pirate language

Learning opportunity: Shows interest in play with language; listens and responds to others; uses language to recreate roles in play situations.

Early Learning Goal: Communication and Language. Listening and attention. Understanding. Speaking.

Resources: Role-play pirate ship or desert island; pirate costumes and accessories; list of pirate sayings and vocabulary.

Key vocabulary: Shiver me timbers, x marks the spot, swashbuckling, high seas, walk the plank, arrr me hearties, grog, bumbo, bounty, plunder, buccaneer, land lubber, bilge rat, scurvy sea dog, land/Ship Ahoy!

Organisation: Joining in with role play.

What to do: As the children play pirates join in and introduce pirate vocabulary and language. Tell them what the different words and sayings mean. For example:

- *Shiver me timbers!:* An expression of surprise meaning 'let my boat break into pieces'.
- *X marks the spot:* Referring to the x on a treasure map.
- *Swashbuckling:* Fighting with swords.
- *High seas:* Open ocean waters.
- *Land/Ship Ahoy!:* There is land or a ship nearby.
- *Walk the plank:* Pirates would tie captured enemies' hands behind their backs and force them to walk blindfolded off a plank into the sea.
- *Arrr me hearties:* Yes my friends.
- *Grog:* Barrels of rum. Pirates also drank 'bumbo', a mixture of rum, water, sugar and nutmeg.
- *Bounty:* Treasure.
- *Plunder:* Violently steal.
- *Buccaneer:* Pirate.
- *Land lubber:* Land lover, someone who stays on land.
- *Bilge rat:* Insult, referring to the rats that lived in the bilge (dirty stinking water) that had collected in the depths of the ship.
- *Scurvy sea dog:* Friendly insult aimed at fellow pirates.

Activity: Composing a pirate sea shanty

Learning opportunity: Enjoys rhyming and rhythmic activities; joins in with repeating refrains; continues a rhyming string.

Early Learning Goal: Literacy. Reading. Writing.

Resources: Whiteboard or flip chart and pen; audio selection of sea shanties.

Key vocabulary: Pirate vocabulary (see 'Pirate language' activity), rhythm, rhyme, beat, clap, sound, describe, listen, sing.

Organisation: Whole group or small groups composing a verse each.

What to do: Listen to a selection of sea shanties (see suggestions in CL, PD and EAD opposite). Sing-a-long and clap the rhythm. Explain that you are going to help the children compose their own pirate sea shanty. Ask them to suggest words and phrases they would like to use in their song. Record their suggestions to create a word bank.

The use the following frame to compose a shanty:

> *Aharr! Aharr! It's a pirate's life for me,*
> *Rocking and swaying on the deep blue sea.*
> *Ahoy! Ahoy! What is that I see?*
> *A ship to be plundered and treasure for me.*

Read this example out and encourage the children to clap along. Repeat it a couple of times to help firmly establish the beat. Then introduce more lines. If needed, give them a prompt, for example:

> *Heave, heave…*

Ask the children what the pirates might be heaving? They may choose sails, in which case can they think of any words to describe the sails billowing in the wind? Or are the pirates in row boats pulling oars?

> *Fire, fire …*

What might the pirates be firing? Can the children suggest any words to describe the sounds of cannons exploding?

Aim to make up four or five verses, then bring the children together and recite them, all the time clapping to the beat. Introduce a tune and turn the rhyme into a song.

Display

Enhance the pirate ship display you made in Theme 1. Invite the children to draw pictures of pirates dancing and stick these onto the deck.

Use a recording device such as the Talking Point from TTS to record the children singing 30 second snippets of sea shanties. Mount these on the display for the children to press and listen to the pirates partying.

Bringing it all together

'Shipwrecked!' role play

Work together to create a role-play shipwreck scene that the children can use as a backdrop for imaginative play.

Preparation

Gather the children and explain that you would like to set up a role-play shipwreck that they can play in. Open a discussion about how a shipwreck might occur.

Together, start to compose a storyline. Ask the children to suggest what might have happened to the ship. Do they know how a ship might sink? Do they have any ideas about how a ship might take on water? If need be, prompt discussion by providing some suggestions: did it run into rocks during a storm? Has it run aground on a desert island? Did an enormous wave tip it over?

Use the storyline as the basis for deciding what the role-play area will need. For example, if the children decide the ship has run aground on a desert island, you will need to create a ship and beach. If they opt for a sinking ship, you will need a half submerged ship and something to represent the water surrounding it.

Ask the children for ideas about what you can use to make the ship, island, water, trees and rocks. Write a list of what you will need.

Create the role-play setting

Involve the children in sourcing objects and materials that can be used to represent the items in the scene. Encourage them to look at shapes, sizes and colours and ask them to consider whether the items they find will adequately serve their intended purposes.

Try charity shops and write home to parents asking if they can provide anything you cannot find. Items that might be useful include: coloured sheets and blankets, tables, chairs, large cardboard boxes, corrugated card, hessian and real rocks and pebbles.

Ask the children to help you set out the scene. For instance, get them to lay out blankets for water, stick green paper leaves on broom handles to make trees and paint cardboard boxes brown like a wooden ship.

Add the detail

Ask the children what kind of props they will need. Source pirate costumes, treasure, chests, spades, telescopes, buckets, ropes, flags, cooking pans, tankards, tools, barrels, bedding/hammocks and a something that can be used as a ship's steering wheel.

Encourage the children to think about how they can enhance the area by creating background scenery. They might like to make or paint pictures of trees, rocks, fish, parrots and animals. Invite them to use the flags they made in Theme 2 and the maps they made in Theme 4.

Play

Give children time to play. Help them to take ownership of the area and think about how they would like to change or improve it. Encourage them to use the pirate language they have learned throughout the topic. Sing the sea shanties composed in Theme 6, use the hats and telescopes made in Theme 3 and the treasure chests made in Theme 5.

Provide craft materials for them to make more treasure to hide around the island and paper for them to write and send SOS messages in bottles.

Observe the children, listen to the different story lines that emerge and continue to provide resources and materials that they can use to enhance their play.

Resources

Resources to collect

- Some museums, libraries and local authorities have collections of unusual objects and musical instruments that they lend out to schools
- Large wooden building blocks and planks, plastic crates, mast and sail set, brooms, clothes airers, ropes, sheets, blankets, white pillow cases, string, buckets
- Coloured, numbered, blank and different-sized pirate flags
- Small world scenes with pirate ships, figures and treasure chests
- Role-play pirate costumes, accessories, chests, glass and plastic jewels, metal and plastic coins, costume jewellery, real coins
- Pirate-themed puzzles, games and numbered dice
- Small hand-held voice recording devices, programmable toys, smart phone or GPS device, metal detectors, microphone.

Everyday resources

- Junk modelling materials; large cardboard boxes, plastic tubs, cardboard containers, shoe boxes, kitchen roll tubes, plastic bottles
- White, black and coloured card, paper, marker pens, pencils, coloured felt pens and pencils, clipboards
- Poster paints and brushes, fabric pens, fabric crayons
- Cellotape, staplers, scissors, hole punch, craft knife, laminator, white stickers
- PE apparatus, climbing frame, gym benches, gym mats, tunnels, slides, tables
- Cones, large balls, bowling pins, hula hoops, beanbags
- Materials and fabrics; corduroy, felt, sandpaper, corrugated card, tinfoil, silk, cellophane
- Playground chalks, salt dough
- Musical instruments
- Different-sized toy plastic boats, spades, bucket scales
- Tinned, jarred, dried, pickled and frozen foods, fresh foods that can be preserved, vinegar, dairy and meat products, cooking chocolate
- Cooking pan, jars, tupperware, chocolate coin moulds
- Dowel rods, petroleum jelly, cement, simple small pulley, cleat, varnish
- Child-sized tools; manual hand drill, vice, screws, screwdriver, measuring tapes.

Information Books

- *Chickens and Pigs (Farmyard Friends)* by Camilla de la Bodoyere
- *Look Inside a Pirate Ship* by Minna Lacey and Stefano Tognetti
- *See Inside: Pirate Ships* by Rob Lloyd Jones and Jorge Muehle
- *Goats (Down on the Farm)* by Sally Morgan

- *Discovering Pirates* by Richard Platt
- *Little Science Stars: Healthy Eating* by Ronnie Randall
- *Know it All: Pirates* by Philip Steele.

Story Books

- *Ten Little Pirates* by Mike Brownlow and Simon Rickerty
- *The Pirates Next Door* and *The Pirate Cruncher* by Jonny Duddle
- *Pirates to the Rescue series* by Tom Easton and Mike Gordon
- *Pirates Love Underpants* by Claire Freedman and Ben Cort
- *The Night Pirates* by Peter Harris and Deborah Allwright
- *Class Three All At Sea* by Julia Jarman and Lynne Chapman
- *On a Pirate Ship* by Anna Millbourne and Benji Davies
- *Pirate Pete* by Nick Sharratt
- *Winnie's Pirate Adventure* by Valerie Thomas and Korky Paul
- *Tim, Ted and the Pirates* by Ian Wybrow.

Websites

- Royal Naval museum: www.royalnavalmuseum.org/info_sheets_piracy.htm
- Royal Museums Greenwich: www.rmg.co.uk/explore/sea-and-ships/all-about/pirates
- Geocaching: www.geocaching.com
- Google Maps: www.google.co.uk/maps

Early years pirates resources and toys

- www.cosydirect.com
- www.yellow-door.net
- www.playmobil.co.uk
- www.tts-group.co.uk

Poems and rhymes

- *Shiver Me Timbers!: Pirate Poems & Paintings* by Douglas Florian and Robert Neubecker
- *Port Side Pirates* by Oscar Seaworthy and Debbi Harter.

Resources for planning

- England: Department for Education (2014) 'Statutory Framework for the Early Years Foundation Stage' (www.foundationyears.org.uk/eyfs-statutory-framwork/)
- Northern Ireland: CCEA (2011) 'Northern Ireland Curriculum' (www.nicurriculum.org.uk/foundation_stage/)
- Scotland: The Scottish Government (2008) 'Curriculum for Excellence' (www.educationscotland.gov.uk/earlyyears/curriculum/index.asp)
- Wales: Welsh Government (2008) 'Framework for children's learning for 3 to 7 year olds in Wales' (http://learning.wales.gov.uk/resources/framework-forchildrens-learning/?skip=1&lang=en).

Collecting evidence of children's learning

Monitoring children's development is an important task. Making a profile of children's achievements, strengths, capabilities interests and learning will help you to see progress and will draw attention to those who are having difficulties for some reason. If a child needs additional professional help, such as speech therapy, these cumulative profiles will provide valuable evidence.

Profiles should cover all the Areas of Learning, as defined by the relevant UK framework, and be the result of collaboration between practitioners, parents and carers. Parents should be made aware of your record keeping policies when their child joins your group. Show parents the types of documentation that you are keeping and make sure they understand their purpose. As a general rule, documentation should be open. Families should have access to their child's documentation at any time and know they can contribute to it. Take regular opportunities to talk to parents about children's progress. If you have formal discussions regarding children about whom you have particular concerns, a dated record of the main points should be kept.

Keeping it manageable

Documentation should be helpful in informing practitioners, adult helpers and parents and always be for the benefit of the child. The golden rule is to keep it simple, manageable and useful. Do not try to make records following every activity!

Documentation will basically fall into two categories – observations and reflections:

Observations

- **Spontaneous observations:** Sometimes you will want to make a note of observations as they happen e.g. a child is heard counting cars accurately during a play activity, or is seen to play collaboratively for the first time.

- **Planned observations:** Sometimes you will plan to make observations of children's developing skills within a planned activity. Using the learning opportunity identified for an activity will help you to make appropriate judgments about children's capabilities, strengths and interests, and to record them systematically.

To collect information:

- Talk to children about their activities and listen to their responses.
- Listen to children talking to each other.
- Observe children's work such as early writing, drawings, paintings and models. (Keeping photocopies or photographs can be useful in tracking progress. Photographs are particularly useful to monitor children's development in the outdoor environment.)

Sometimes it may be appropriate to set up 'one off' activities for the purposes of monitoring development. Some groups at the beginning of each term, for example, ask children to write their name and to make a drawing of themselves to record their progressing skills in both co-ordination and observation.

Reflections

It is useful to spend regular time reflecting on the children's progress. Aim to make some comments about each child each week, and discuss these regularly with colleagues and families.

Informing your planning

Collecting evidence about children's progress is time consuming and it is important that it is useful. When planning, use the information collected to help you to decide what learning opportunities you need to provide next for each child. For example, a child who has poor pencil or brush control will benefit from more play with dough or construction toys to build strength of muscles in the hands and fingers.

Example observation sheet

Name: Lucy Field

Date: 17.1.13

Area of Learning: Mathematics. Count reliably with numbers from 1 to 20.

Context (Please tick):

Child-initiated: √   **Adult-led:**

Alone: **In a group:** √

Observation: Lucy is playing outside with two friends. She is trying to build the tallest tower and counting the bricks. "1, 2, 3, 4, 5, 7, 8. Mine's 8. Yours is only 7." She knocks the tower down, chuckles and starts to build again, counting as she places the bricks. "1, 2, 3, 4, 5, 7." The tower falls over. "Oh blow. I wanted to do 20."

What next: Check Lucy knows 6 follows 5. Encourage use of the outdoor counting grids, skittles and number rhyme CD.

Observer: E. M. Hogg

Overview of areas covered through 'Pirates'

	Communication and Language	Physical Development	Personal, Social and Emotional Development	Literacy	Mathematics	Understanding the World	Expressive Arts and Design
Ship Ahoy!	Listening and attention Understanding Speaking	Moving and handling Health and self-care	Self-confidence and self-awareness Managing feelings and behaviour Making relationships	Reading Writing	Numbers Shape, space and measures	People and communities The world Technology	Exploring and using media and materials Being imaginative
Flying the Jolly Roger flag	Listening and attention Understanding Speaking	Moving and handling Health and self-care	Self-confidence and self-awareness Managing feelings and behaviour Making relationships	Reading Writing	Numbers Shape, space and measures	People and communities The world Technology	Exploring and using media and materials Being imaginative
A pirate's life	Listening and attention Understanding Speaking	Moving and handling Health and self-care	Self-confidence and self-awareness Managing feelings and behaviour Making relationships	Reading Writing	Numbers Shape, space and measures	People and communities The world Technology	Exploring and using media and materials Being imaginative
'X marks the spot'	Listening and attention Understanding Speaking	Moving and handling Health and self-care	Self-confidence and self-awareness Managing feelings and behaviour Making relationships	Reading Writing	Numbers Shape, space and measures	People and communities The world Technology	Exploring and using media and materials Being imaginative
Buried treasure	Listening and attention Understanding Speaking	Moving and handling Health and self-care	Self-confidence and self-awareness Managing feelings and behaviour Making relationships	Reading Writing	Numbers Shape, space and measures	People and communities The world Technology	Exploring and using media and materials Being imaginative
Sea shanties	Listening and attention Understanding Speaking	Moving and handling Health and self-care	Self-confidence and self-awareness Managing feelings and behaviour Making relationships	Reading Writing	Numbers Shape, space and measures	People and communities The world Technology	Exploring and using media and materials Being imaginative

Note: For each theme, highlight the Early Learning Goal areas covered through both adult focused and child-initiated activities relating to 'Pirates'.

Home links

The theme of 'Pirates' lends itself to useful links with children's homes and families. Through working together, children and adults gain respect for each other and build comfortable and confident relationships.

Establishing partnerships
● Keep parents informed about the themes for 'Pirates' and the activities for each week. By understanding the work of the group, parents can get involved by contributing ideas, time and resources.
● Photocopy the 'Family page' for each child to take home.
● Invite children to bring in books about pirates from home.
● Send home a treasure chest for the children to fill with personal treasures. Explain that these treasures should have sentimental value. On their return to the setting, invite each child to go through their chest and talk through the contents.
● Invite children to bring in their role-play pirate costumes from home. Remember to ask parents to ensure everything is clearly named.
● Find out what museums and exhibitions there are in your local area. Put this information together on a fact sheet and hand it out to parents to give them ideas about where to take their children to learn more about pirates.
● Lend out pirate stories for children to share with their parents at home.

Visiting enthusiasts
● Find out if there is an education officer at a local museum who is willing to visit and bring in some pirate artefacts for the children to see.
● Invite families involved in farming or food production to bring in some produce from animals that would have been kept on a pirate ship, for example, eggs, pork and goats cheese, and tell the children a bit about how it is produced.

Resource requests
● Ask parents to contribute clean food and household packaging that the children can use for junk modelling.
● See if they can donate or lend some old costume jewellery, sheets, pillowcases, blankets, ropes, hessian sacks, pebbles, large cardboard boxes, buckets, tankards or barrels to your setting.
● Ask parents if they can make pirate hats, treasure, flags and telescopes with their children and send them in to be used in the role-play area.